ENDORSEMENTS

Twenty-six years ago when I first started the journey of ministry, someone said these words to me and they have stayed with me until this day, "Every success is a prayer success and every failure is a prayer failure." A.R.M.E.D is so much more than a manuscript and manual, it's a masterpiece! The church is so busy singing and preaching that we have lost the art of intercession.

Bettis-Davis has penned the heart of God as it relates to strategic, powerful, and productive prayer. This script is filled with revelation and insight. It is a **must** for today's church.

Apostle Kevin Mihlfeld
New Hope Christian Center
Tallahassee, Florida

* * *

Apostle Karen Bettis-Davis is a present-day Apostolic General, whose life and ministry reflects the authentic leadership tempered by a deep compassion for not only the Body of Christ, but the world at large. Birthed, transformed, equipped, and transitioned at battling the very enemy of our soul, God has strategically placed her, not only as an arrow in the hand of a warrior, but He has anointed and empowered her to be a weapon of mass destruction. She possesses years of experience through knowledge and effective application of the scriptures, spiritual warfare, and intercession.

I've witnessed her leading people out of deep depression, life-threatening illnesses, mental and emotional breakdowns, and legal situations utilizing the very methods outlined in this book. For this cause, she has been **sent** and set! Apostle Karen Bettis-Davis is a FEARLESS Warrior! No doubt, she will leave a footprint in the earth for the Kingdom of God that can never be erased. Prepare to be ***A.R.M.E.D!***

Apostle Karen Register-Veney
Kingdom Demonstration Ministries
Tappahannock, Virginia

We're living in a crucial hour! We're living in a time when Heaven is groaning for the sons and daughters of God to wake up and cry out to God. We're living in a time where our prayers can't just be emotional, they have to be intentional, and most of all, **strategic.**

In her new book, Apostle Bettis-Davis carefully and ingeniously creates a blueprint for prayer! She teaches the reader how to strategically engage Heaven when pulling down the strongholds, systems, and structures of the enemy! This book is not only needed in this hour, but it is also a powerful read that will transcend time to reach future generations because the revelation, strategies, and information shared in this masterpiece are timeless!

You need this book; this book is invaluable! Apostle Bettis-Davis did a wonderful job interweaving all of the elements needed to not only successfully engage in warfare, but to **win in warfare!** This book is a must-have for every prayer warrior, creative, and leader! **It will definitely upgrade your prayer life!**

Apostle Bryan Meadows
Founder, Senior Leader
Embassy International Worship Center
Atlanta, Georgia

FOREWORD

I remember when I first met Apostle Karen Davis—it was at the Dale City Christian Center. We were having a missions conference and she was serving the pulpit. I remember how she served so faithfully and how she also worshipped so phenomenally. That day, God had me speak a prophetic word into her life about her worship and the way in which she served would get her in trouble as others will become jealous. I told her to keep worshipping and keep serving. That day I realized the anointing upon her life and how God was going to bless that anointing. I knew it was going to lead her into great places. Now, it has come into fruition as she has established her church and it's blessing so many people. Her personal ministry has even gone beyond the borders of Rehoboth and it has also blessed many people around the country. Now, her book *A.R.M.E.D,* is poised to go even farther. Not only is this her book going to bless people around the country, but it's going to bless people around the world. I believe the anointing from her worship and her service has enabled her to identify how this specific prayer need is so important for the lives of God's people. I'm excited to see its impact on the current and emerging generation of intercessors.

A.R.M.E.D is a must-read for those who are ready to engage the enemy or take their engagement of the enemy to a new level! In this manuscript, Apostle Karen Bettis-Davis offers us a unique and bold approach that causes a sleeping giant to awake and live out purpose as spiritual warring people under the leadership of generals who are appointed by the great General, Jesus Christ our Lord.

Bettis-Davis outlines a formula for orderly warfare intercession as we thread our way through a systematic approach towards spiritual victory in our lives as believers, for our church, for our cities, for our state, region, and our nation. These individual victories are not just for the individuals' comfort but the advancement of the Kingdom of God first and then as a soldier in the army of the Lord.

This book walks the intercessor through transitioning from the ACTS Prayer model to the ***A.R.M.E.D*** Prayer model. It takes the believer from a defensive posture to an offensive posture. In addition to effectively against warring against satanic attacks, the believer will be able to reclaim territories from the enemy and re-establish Kingdom territory. Parts of this book may upset you as Bettis-Davis seems aggressive in her determination to war for God, but I say to you don't get upset, get ***A.R.M.E.D!*** Apostle Bettis-Davis has issued a clarion call to the Body of Christ to war.

Bettis-Davis is calling us to be strong in the Lord and the power of His might. You hear her heart for intercessors and believers to exercise our rights as Kingdom warriors. Jesus Christ has done His part by setting us free, now we must do our part to stay free and set others free. When you complete this "How to" intercessory warfare manual, **you will be *A.R.M.E.D* and ready for war!**

Bishop Nathaniel Gomillion
Tabernacle of Praise FGBC
Zuni, Virginia
Bishop of Emerging Churches &
Fellowship Assistance
Full Gospel

Introduction

The Vision of a Mighty Army

Early one morning God took me up in a vision. It captivated everything within me. It was as if I was there. It was a powerful vision of a great and vast army. They were in a war sequence with their general initiating the charge. One particular warrior was skillful, calculated, and prepared. Her soldiers were ready to follow her every command and they were well able to strike a deadly blow to her enemies. I was swept into the middle of this vision by a powerful force, which caught me up into the heavens like a forceful vacuum sucking everything into its chambers. All of a sudden, the air drew itself back as if in anticipation of the beginning of an epic battle. I looked up and the women warriors were bruised, and they were battered, but they were still "fierce." Then, one of the warriors who had been running with the speed of a gazelle appeared. She took out her sword, fixed her eyes on her target and took a GIANT LEAP in preparation to strike.

It felt like EVERYTHING stopped in anticipation of the blow she was about to give to her enemy. As she drew back with all of her apostolic might the atmosphere gathered itself to flow in concert with her. She ascended high into the heavens. The wind had taken her up. The clouds surrounded WITH HER. That army followed her lead and took the same position. They synchronized themselves to make ONE STRIKING BLOW TOGETHER.

ANGELS were mounted on top of their horses. This scene showed legions and legions of angels so thick you'd almost missed the clouds. **They were assembling. They were preparing. They were together.** Heaven had backed them! They were about to give the enemy the blow that God had intended in the garden when he said:" *And I will put enmity between thee and the woman, and between thy seed and her seed; it shall bruise thy head, and thou shalt bruise his heel." (Genesis 3:15, KJV)*

THE SONS AND DAUGHTERS of Eve are prepared! They are focused! We are battle-tested! We are determined! Our hearts are fixed! **LET'S STRIKE THE BLOW!!!!!**

***

We all have a war cadence (a rhythmical flow/pattern; a habit or systematic way of moving) we are supposed to surrender to God. In 2018, the Lord began to speak to me about prayer. When you begin to measure a society, when you look at what's happening in the world, you look at what's happening in the church, it looks as if the world is winning. It seems as if that there are people who were once believers, are now atheists. There are people who were once die-hard Christians who have converted to Islam. We are now seeing physical churches that have been inhabited by Christians for hundreds of years being converted into mosques; especially in the large metropolitan areas like DC. Places that were once erected and dedicated for the sole purpose of worshipping God are no longer the houses of God.

So, I began to ask God: what is happening here? How can the enemy be so bold as to step right before our faces? How can we have been so deceived to where we are now "selling" holy ground to the highest bidder? How it is so easy to make merchandise of something that belongs to God? What is happening? God's response to me: **We need to change the formula for prayer.**

The Need for a New Model

Now tell the truth, when you were growing up, how many people learned the "ACTS" model of prayer? The "A" stands for "adoration." The C stands for "confession." The "T" stands for "thanksgiving" and the "S" stands for supplication. The earliest printed example I have found specifically referring to the acronym ACTS is from a serial story by Marion Harland (Mary Virginia Terhune) which was printed in an August 8, 1883 publication of the, *The Continent: "Our Mr. Burgess once informed a youth theologue in my hearing that 'the monosyllable,' ACTS, formed an excellent epitomical guide in the composition of the principal prayer offered in public worship. This should begin with Adoration, proceed to Confession, rise into Thanksgiving and close with Supplication."* Mr. Burgess is the name of the pastor in the story; however, the author's husband was a Presbyterian minister, Edward Payson Terhune. So if the acronym was not original to her, it's possible that she picked it up from him. Earlier authors referred to the same four elements in the same sequence but did not mention an acronym. For example, the *Principles of Christian Philosophy (1836)* includes: "*Generally speaking, prayer may be arranged under the heads of adoration, confession, thanksgiving, and supplication.*" **We've been using this model since 1836!**

Essentially, this model of prayer is about a living relationship with God but guess what? In that specific model, **there's no room for warfare.** Think about it. You've been praying a model that actually positions a target on your back. It identifies you as God's child, but you have no weapons, you do not acknowledge the more critical battle in heavenly places, and there no place of defeat for the enemy. You've been praying a model that does not engage angels. It does not apply the blood of Jesus and it does not provoke you to use your authority. However, this model does cause you to be a standing target for the enemy. As I did my research for this book, I found that many, many churches still teach and use this model as a basis for social and private prayer. They refer to it often as the model that Jesus prayed in **Matthew 6:9-13**. However, the last thing Jesus says is "**thy kingdom come, on earth as it is in heaven**." Well, the Apostle Paul and other holy men of God who wrote the inspired Word of God, tell us about epic battles that occur in the heavenly places. Daniel, Isaiah, Ezekiel, and others were actual witnesses to the war in the heavenlies. The Apostle Paul then charges us that **here is where we must also engage—in the heavenlies**. This realization leaves me with one conclusion: **it is time for a new formula for prayer. IT'S TIME TO STRIKE THE BLOW!**

CHAPTER 1

HARDWIRED FOR WAR

I grew up the only daughter of a Sargent Major in the United States Army and our family lived all over the world. Rank and order were always around me. Executing a task for a greater mission is what I was raised to do. The invisible goal of peace and protection was interwoven throughout every fiber of my being. As a child, I was very aware that my idea of safety and security was much different from my friends who came from non-military families. Order was ingrained into the very fabric of every aspect of our lives. My brothers and I knew how our actions affected our father's career and we also learned how my father's career impacted the entire nation. Even as children, we were taught that every decision we made had its own set of consequences. Our decisions could not only impact our father, but they could also impact my father's commanding officer, as well as the entire base. We were taught the rules of conduct, especially when we lived on foreign soil.

War was all around us, but military families are truly the ones who understand war and its consequences. Gaining access to a military base teaches you a lot about the duties of watchmen. An MPS's (Military Police) job is to stand guard at the gates in order to protect and defend not only those who live inside the gates, but their job is also to protect and serve those inside the gates so that peace and order is maintained. Guards and gates were normal parts of our military lives, so were the sounds of war. The endless cannons going off during training drills or to what we often referred to, as "maneuvers" were very common. On an active military base, we were used to peacetime training based on wartime missions. The base was always preparing for a war—*always*.

Keeping C-Rations or MRE's (Meals Ready to Eat) in our homes in case of an emergency was just a normal part of our lives. We were given MRE's as snacks, but we understood that these meals would give us our daily sustenance if a war were to ever come to our soil. We were to use these to survive on until the Calvary arrived. I had many friends who could not even begin to understand the nuances of military life. Watching my father gave me a perspective on making great sacrifices for God and country in a way that gave me great pride. I was proud to be the daughter of a man who played a vital role in the securing of a nation. I understood that his career had great impact on not just him, but our family, as well as our nation—that was at times both difficult and rewarding. Having grown up with a military parent, I understand what an impact a military life can have on a person all too well; and that impact could be extremely difficult at times. I also realized that growing up with a military parent helped me to understand the role of God as Commander in Chief and my role as a soldier in **His Great Army.**

I was proud to be the daughter of a man who played a vital role in the securing of a nation.

As the child of a military Sargent Major we had a few hard and fast rules that we were expected to live by:

1) **LIVE IN ORDER.** There was never a time when we were allowed to have our home unkept. Order was expected in every room and in every corner of our home. Inspections were a regular occurrence in our home. We were taught to keep order.

2) **ROUTINES AND INSTRUCTIONS.** These were commonplace. Children need routines and structure in order to feel safe. We had certain routines that we were expected to follow whether my dad was home to watch us or not. Those routines kept us safe and accounted for.

3) **RESPECT AT ALL TIMES.** There was never a moment where adults, teachers, police officers, preachers, or any ruling authority were to be disrespected. **We were taught to respect even our enemies.** We were taught to be diplomatic and authoritative but to never disrespect the rank or anyone's power. Generals don't always wear their uniform; sometimes not even on the inside of a base. So giving respect as a general rule kept you from dishonoring those whose rank deserves honor.

4) **MATURITY AND RESILIENCE**. Maturity is an asset that often goes hand in hand with flexibility. Military families often cope with difficult situations such as deployment. Separation from family and friends is a part of military life and these events enable us to pursue new experiences and develop skills one may not have otherwise.

5) **EDUCATION IS ESSENTIAL.** I witnessed my father enroll in continuing education courses his entire career. He was always training for his next assignment and promotion. If you were going to be promoted, you needed to take as many courses pertaining to your MOS Code (Military Occupational Specialty Code). An MOS Code is a nine-character code used in the United States Army and United States Marine Corps to identify a specific job. So, we learned that training and continuing education was the key to advancement.

Other valuable skills I learned: there was no job beneath you; there is no substitute for hard work; relationships are invaluable; history matters; and war is inevitable—**so you must learn how to skillfully wage war.** My father saw everything from a battle matrix. Life was about good overcoming evil, winning over losing, and freedom over captivity. He taught us that wars have a higher purpose than the safety of the individual soldier. Wars bring peace to all who are citizens of the winning nation or kingdom.

Today we find that many spiritual warfare modules focus on the individual who is personally struggling with a weakness of his own flesh and often mislabel a personal hardship as spiritual battle. We often teach that a spiritual battle is about the comfort of the individual rather than enmity against the enemies of God—which are princes, rulers, the authorities, the powers of this dark world; and the spiritual forces of evil in the heavenly realms. Many manuals promise deliverance from the weariness of life's individual battles, but this is quite the opposite of the type of training a soldier may receive in our nation's armed forces. Although each individual soldier must be trained to survive on a battlefield, most of his training concerned **accomplishing the mission and defeating an enemy. Defeat happens by fighting as a member of a team under the orders of a chain of command.**

There is a cadence to proper warfare, and it does not lend itself to lone ranger strategies and simply using our natural visible soldiers in battle. Such ego-centered warfare has led to many causalities of war.

The Body of Christ must learn how to lock arms and gather troops in order to defeat the enemies of our God and advance. We need every rank, every level, and every believer to learn not only how to engage in battle at your level, but also how to strategize with soldiers against the schemes of the enemy by taking our orders from our Commander and Chief in order for the kingdoms of this world to become the kingdoms of our Lord and of His Christ. We must create a model of prayer that actually engages and deposes the enemies that oppose us all because of our King. **Amen.**

CHAPTER 2

THE UNSEEN REALM

Billy Graham explained the reality of spiritual warfare in his book, *Angels:*

"We live in a perpetual battlefield…the wars among the nations on earth are mere popgun affairs compared to the fierceness of battle in the spiritual unseen world. This invisible spiritual conflict is waged around us incessantly and unremittingly. Where the Lord works, Satan's forces hinder; where angel beings carry out divine directives, the devils rage. All this comes about because the powers of darkness press their counterattack to recapture the ground held for the glory of God…

Since the fall of Lucifer, the angel of light, and son of the morning—there has been no respite in the bitter battle of the Ages. Night and day Lucifer, the master craftsman of the devices of darkness, labors to thwart God's plan of the ages. We can find inscribed on every page of human history the consequences of the evil brought to fruition by the powers of darkness with the devil in charge. Satan never yields an inch, nor does he ever pause in his opposition to the plan of God to redeem the "cosmos" from his control."

We live in a world inhabited by invisible beings. This world is filled with functional, invisible beings. The spirit world is alive, vibrant, moving, and causing things to occur within the natural realm.

> Humans are given five traditional senses to help us experience the world around us.

They are all around us yet not immediately obvious to many since the visible realm is so much more imposing. Humans are given five traditional senses to help us experience the world around us. **Those five senses are: sight, hearing, smell, touch, and taste.** Each of these five senses consists of organs that are receptors. The stimuli from each sensing organ in the body are relayed to different parts of the brain through various pathways. Just as we have senses in the natural that connect to the visible world, we have spiritual senses that connect us to the spiritual world. In the natural, we predominantly use hearing and seeing as the senses we filter life through. In the spiritual realm, we use these same receptors except we use the gift of discerning of spirits to help us locate and identify which spirits we re-engage with. The spiritual sense of seeing is our capacity to discern the reality of the spirit world, which lies in the back of every form, symbol, experience, word, and action. This seeing begins in prayer. Our faith is what makes what is invisible—VISIBLE.

In **2 Kings 6:15-17**, the prophet Elisha's servant saw something in the visible realm that overwhelmed him—the Syrian army encircling their city with horses and chariots. *"Alas, my master!"* he said. *"What shall we do?"*

Elisha, though not shaken, saw a deeper reality in the unseen realm.

"Do not fear, for those who are with us are more than those who are with them. Elisha then prayed and said, "O Lord, I pray, open his eyes that he may see." And the Lord opened the servant's eyes and he saw. And behold, the mountain was full of horses and chariots of fire all around Elisha."

Elisha saw something his servant did not see: the enemies of God surrounding the city were themselves surrounded by a massive invisible army assembled and ready to fight on their behalf behind the scenes for Elisha's protection. The prophet was able to see the unseen. The power to see in the spirit is peculiar to our faith in Christ. The power to see in the spirit is both a gift and a weapon. I liken it to the night-vision goggles that military soldiers may wear when they go on a reconnaissance mission at night while it's dark. They are able to see clearly during the time where others cannot.

Reconnaissance is the act of reconnoitering (to make a military observation) specially to gain information about an enemy or potential enemy.

CHAPTER 3

ARMED & DANGEROUS

The Bible says that *the kingdoms of this world shall become the kingdoms of our Lord and of his Christ*, **Revelations 11:15**. This means that we are all a part of an army and we each have a rank in that army. This translates to the fact that we all have duties. All of us have regions, we have battle stations, and we have particular places where we are called to rule and to subdue the enemy. In **Genesis,** He said this: we like to talk about the fact that we're supposed to have dominion, but you can never have dominion without a fight. There is never an enemy on the face of the earth, above it, or beneath it that will ever surrender without a battle.

We've been in our pulpits, we've been conducting our workshops, and we've been on our *Facebook Lives* sowing the demonic scheme that the church is a hospital. WRONG. The church is a **war room.** Now, we have got to shift our mindsets and begin to think of prayer as a weapon. We have to think of intercession as a weapon, as a duty, as a calling, and as a rank – an **MOS (Military Operation Specialty)** in the church. In the army, an MOS is a duty or related group of duties that a soldier by training, skill, and experience is best qualified to perform; that is a basis for the classification, assignment, and advancement of enlisted personnel.

It took one woman to cause the world to be in a fallen state. But if we were to all band together and use our power, our authority, our various skill sets, our ranks, our positions—essentially, use everything that God has placed on the inside of us, we could *literally*

> "If the first woman God ever made, was strong enough to turn the world upside down, all alone (referring to Eve of the Bible), then these women together ought to be able to turn it back and get it right side up again."
>
> – Sojourner Truth

turn the world right-side up. Everybody's waiting for Jesus to come down and do it, but Jesus already said, *"it is finished,"* **John 19:30**. He says: I'm sitting and I'm measuring **you.** I'm watching **you.** I'm observing how **you** handle this weapon called prayer. You do realize that our God is the only prayer-answering God that exists? You do understand that every other religion is void of an authentic, supernatural God? A sovereign King? Let's be clear, other religions do not have a God who is the God of angel armies. **But our God does indeed have an army.**

I want to reference the perspective of Debra. Judges 5:1-3, *Then Deborah and Barak the son of Abinoam sang on that day, saying: When leaders lead in Israel, when the people willingly offer themselves, Bless the Lord! "Hear, O kings! Give ear, O princes! I, even I, will sing to the Lord; I will sing praise to the Lord God of Israel.*

The first thing we see is that worship is also a weapon. **Your praise is a weapon.** I know we often do a lot of dancing. We do a lot of bucking and we do a lot of sweating. We practice our dances and we do all these things during our services. But honestly, if praise could save the church, Jesus would have been back by now. If praise were ALL we needed to usher in our King, Jesus would have been back! But he says, NO! You are here to subdue kingdoms. There are two things God wants. He wants: **1) gods and he wants 2) nations.** He wants every other god to be made low and He wants the people of every nation to come back to Him. That's our mandate on the earth. We must **subdue gods** and **turn people back to God**. So, here we see that worship is a weapon.

Then the scripture goes on to talk about the days when the highways were abandoned and the villagers in Israel would not fight. Verse 7 says *they held back until I, Deborah arose until I arose a mother in Zion.* Are you willing to take responsibility for your community? For your region? How about your neighborhood or the street you live on?

What about the children in the house who live two doors down from you? Are you willing to fight and take back your AUTHORITY? So Deborah says, *"I arose as a mother in Zion."* God chose new leaders when war came to the city's gates, but not a shield or spear was seen among the 40,000 in Israel.

Who's fighting? This verse says: *my heart is with Israel's princes.* Travelers took to winding paths. This means that they were scared and because of their fear, they decided to take an alternative route instead of going straight at the enemy and taking the fight directly to him. The Bible reads, "My heart was Israel's priests." The travelers who took the **winding road** means that the villagers in Israel would not fight.

Somehow the church has started taking "winding roads" and now we pray **powerless prayers expecting God to do the work he commissioned us to do.** God is not moved by any of that because He knows what He's placed on the inside of you. He knows He's given you power, He knows He's given you authority and He's assigned angels to back you.

***

It is time for us to arise. It was out of this revelation the kingdom's need for this new method of prayer was birthed. It's time for us to become **ARMED** and strike a blow!

A.R.M.E.D STANDS FOR:

A: Affirmation, Admiration & Applying the Blood of Jesus
R: Repentance, Reconciliation and Redress.
M: Meditation on the scriptures
E: Employing and engaging in Warfare
D: Destroy the works of the devil

A.R.M.E.D. is a prototype for prayer that allows *every* believer to engage in the Christ-given mandate to defeat the enemies of our God and His Kingdom.

The following are a few reference scriptures that gives us permission and authority to operate in spiritual warfare and intercession:

- *When the enemy shall come in like a flood, the Spirit of the LORD shall lift up a standard against him.* **Isaiah 59:19**
- *He gave them power against unclean spirits, to cast them out, and to heal all manner of sickness and all manner of disease.* **Matthew 10:1**
- *And I will give unto thee the keys of the kingdom of heaven: and whatsoever thou shalt bind on earth shall be bound in heaven: and whatsoever thou shalt loose on earth shall be loosed in heaven.* **Matthew 16:19**
- *Get thee behind me, Satan: for thou savourest not the things that be of God, but the things that be of men.* **Mark 8:33**
- *Then he called his twelve disciples together, and gave them power and authority over all devils, and to cure diseases.* **Luke 9:1**
- *Lord even the devils are subject unto us through thy name.* **Luke 10:17**

- *Behold, I give unto you power to tread on serpents and scorpions, and over all the power of the enemy: and nothing shall by any means hurt you.* **Luke 10:19**

- *(For the weapons of our warfare are not carnal, but mighty through God to the pulling down of strong holds;) Casting down imaginations, and every high thing that exalts itself against the knowledge of God, and bringing into captivity every thought to the obedience of Christ;* **2 Corinthians 10:4,5**

- *Neither give place to the devil.* **Ephesians 4:27**

- *Finally, my brethren, be strong in the Lord, and in the power of his might. Put on the whole amour of God, that ye may be able to stand against the wiles of the devil.* **Ephesians 6:10, 11**

- *Be sober, be vigilant; because your adversary the devil, as a roaring lion, walketh about, seeking whom he may devour: Whom resist steadfast in the faith.* **1 Peter 5:8,9**

- *For this purpose, the Son of God was manifested, that he might destroy the works of the devil.* **1 John 3:8**

- *Ye are of God, little children, and have overcome them: because greater is he that is in you, than he that is in the world.* **1 John 4:4**

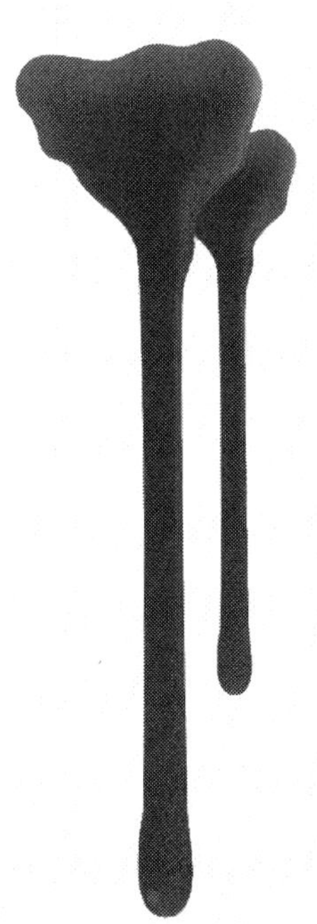

CHAPTER 4

A - AFFIRMATION, ADMIRATION, APPLYING THE BLOOD OF JESUS

When you go into prayer, the first act you must do is begin to **love on God. Love on your heavenly Father.** You must go into your chamber; your most sacred and secret place. Become intimate with God; have intercourse and discourse with God. Worship God and become one with your Father. You must affirm Him as the Lord over your life and as the **commander-in-chief** who is sending you into battle. You must go into your chamber knowing that He gave you the power to become a Son of God. You must go into prayer knowing that you have a right to access the throne room and you have a responsibility to **depose** enemies.

There are generations on your shoulders and there are regions looking for you. God just doesn't put churches in certain places just because He wants to have a church on every corner. God is very strategic with placing specific churches where He places them. This occurs because there are principalities and spiritual wickedness in high places in strategic areas. There are demons and there are powers working and it is *your* job to depose them. Battalions of intercessors in every region must arise and stand up placing the banner of Jesus Christ in the ground in order to make a declaration to **every enemy of God.** This declaration is to either give up—**or die.**

Every enemy of God needs to be placed on notice. We should hang up warning posters as they did in the Old West when there was a bounty placed on the criminals of that time. We should include an inscription that says: "We're not going to stop until we stop you! We're not going to stop until you've gone back to hell where you've come from! We're not going to stop until we see an increase in the glory of God. We're not going to stop until we see a decrease in murders, drug addictions, unwed mothers, and pregnancies out of wedlock. We're not going to stop until you're out of there! You are WANTED by the Sons of God and **we are here to hunt you down!**

AFFIRM YOURSELF IN GOD

You must have courage in order to enter into warfare. I've heard some people say that "warfare is not for everybody" – the devil is a liar. That notion is the trick of the devil devised to disarm you and to attempt to get you to lay down your weapons. **Everyone has a**

responsibility to war. According to **Genesis 1:26-28** we have a responsibility to take dominion. The moment we enter into our new life in Christ, the enemies of our God also become our enemies. We must understand and take up the duties and responsibilities of a solider in The Lord's army. You were created to dominate at every level of maturity in Christ. Intercession and spiritual warfare are the responsibility of *every* born-again believer. The Bible tells us that men should always pray.

1 Then He spoke a parable to them, that men always ought to pray and not lose heart, 2 saying: "There was in a certain city a judge who did not fear God nor regard man. 3 Now there was a widow in that city; and she came to him, saying, 'Get justice for me from my adversary.' 4 And he would not for a while; but afterward he said within himself, 'Though I do not fear God nor regard man, 5 yet because this widow troubles me I will avenge her, lest by her continual coming she weary me.'" 6 Then the Lord said, "Hear what the unjust judge said. 7 And shall God not avenge His own elect who cry out day and night to Him, though He bears long with them? 8 I tell you that He will avenge them speedily. Nevertheless, when the Son of Man comes, will He really find faith on the earth?" Luke 18:1-8

Here we are specifically told: "that men always ought to pray and not lose heart." The scripture is clearly telling us that prayer is a choice. We must choose to pray. Many times, when we find ourselves in despair it can simply be because we chose not to pray. Either pray or lose heart. If I pray as Jesus taught I should, in His name and with the weapons at my disposal, and an obedient faith, I will not lose heart! Praying in faith and with the right weapons will not only lead us to victory but it will also keep us with a renewed hope. When the enemy attacks we must all choose to pray or lose heart. Jesus gives a reason why we should always pray. In this passage He is calling attention to an unjust judge saying "if an evil judge will eventually give relief, how much more will God bring relief to those who call upon him?" He is saying, **PRAY! I WILL RESPOND!**

Either pray or lose heart.

AFFIRM YOUR POSITION IN CHRIST

You will bring God glory when you accept and welcome one another as partners, just as the Anointed One has fully accepted you and received you as his partner. Romans 15:7 TPT

Look with wonder at the depth of the Father's marvelous love that he has lavished on us! He has called us and made us his very own beloved children. The reason the world doesn't recognize who we are is that they didn't recognize him. Beloved, we are God's children right now; however, it is not yet apparent what we will become. But we do know that when it is finally made visible, we will be just like him, for we will see him as he truly is. 1 John 3:1-2 TPT

You didn't choose me, but I've chosen and commissioned you to go into the world to bear fruit. And your fruit will last, because whatever you ask of my Father, for my sake, he will give it to you! John 15:16 TPT

AFFIRM YOUR RIGHT TO WAR

I thank you, God, for making me so mysteriously complex! Everything you do is marvelously breathtaking. It simply amazes me to think about it! How thoroughly you know me, Lord! Psalm 139:14 TPT

But those who embraced him and took hold of his name p were given authority to become the children of God! John 1:12 TPT

Have you forgotten that your body is now the sacred temple of the Spirit of Holiness, who lives in you? You don't belong to yourself any longer, for the gift of God, the Holy Spirit, lives inside your sanctuary. You were God's expensive purchase, paid for with tears of blood, so by all means, then, use your body to bring glory to God! 1 Corinthians 6:19-20 TPT

I have never called you 'servants,' because a master doesn't confide in his servants, and servants don't always understand what the master is doing. But I call you my most intimate friends, for I reveal to you everything that I've heard from my Father. John 15:15 TPT

***

Who stole your stuff? Who told you that there was no fight in you? Who told you that whatever the enemy takes, it's his to have? Who told you that lie? Who made you believe that you are not a weapon in the hands of your God? The Holy Ghost comes into each of us and teaches us how to war. As believers we have victory in spiritual warfare by counting ourselves as dead, crucified with Christ, and that the life we live is not our own, but Christ living through us. Our lives should manifest Jesus Christ as He continues His work in this world through us defeating the devil's strongholds, strategizing to defeat his schemes, and destroying the works of the devil, of the world systems, and of the carnal flesh.

DECLARE THIS:

I can see the Kingdom of God because I am born again. John 3:3

I don't worry about everyday life. God knows my needs and meets them because I make His Kingdom my primary concern. Matthew 6:25-33

Jesus shows himself to me because I love him. John 14:21

Because Jesus died for my sins, I am no longer separated from God. I live in close union with him. Romans 5:10

The fruit I produce brings great joy to God, my Father in Heaven. John 15:8

God's power works best in my weakness. 2 Corinthians 12:9

Through the energy of Christ working powerfully in me, I teach others His truths. Colossians 1:29

I have been saved, not by works, but grace, so that I might do good works. Ephesians 2:9-10

My faith makes me whole in spirit, soul and body. Mark 5:34

When I call out to God He answers me. He tells me things I wouldn't know otherwise. Jeremiah 33:3

Because I place my hope in the Lord my strength is renewed. Isaiah 40:31

As I follow Jesus…as I walk with him, I have peace. Luke 24:36

Because I obey Jesus I remain in his love. John 15:10

The cross of Christ is my power. 1 Corinthians 1:17

My God meets all my needs. Philippians 4:19

God is my refuge and strength…always ready to help me in times of trouble. Psalm 46:1

So, we love on God and then we apply the **Blood of Jesus.**

APPLYING THE BLOOD OF JESUS: OUR PRAYER

The Blood is your cover and your weapon, your advocate and your Intercessor. The blood of Jesus is essential for defeating the enemy, dealing with accusations, stopping premature death, and healing your natural body. You must apply the blood of Jesus when you're going into warfare. I think one of the things that we don't realize is the blood of Jesus is an **intercessor**. It is a warrior. It speaks for us. It covers and protects. We don't apply the blood of Jesus enough anymore in the church. We don't talk about the blood of Jesus enough and the power of the eternal power from the blood of Jesus. Therefore, when you're going into warfare, you must apply the **blood of Jesus.**

Prayer example using the Blood of Jesus:

We've come in the name of the Lord of hosts, Jehovah Sabaoth. We've come to destroy the demonic powers of the princes over the land, over the city, over the state, and over our nation. So we declare and know, that the Lord of hosts and his body who do battle for the saints, his body, his kingdom. And we will take no prisoners, but this body army will not stop. We are on the offensive until it is time to see our savior face to face. So we say ARISE, ARISE! For the Lord has given us cities. The Lord has given us lands. The Lord has given us states and the Lord has given us nations by the blood of Jesus Christ. Our sins are forgiven through the blood. We are given life, abundant life through the blood! We now dwell in Christ and He is in us by the blood.

Jesus is our atonement by His blood. We are justified by the blood. We are saved for ransom by the blood. We have access to come near to God by the blood. We are given peace by the blood. We are reconciled to God by the blood. The blood of God is a peacemaker. God is our arbitrator. We use the blood to bathe and to heal each cell. We immerse ourselves in the proper fluids and we put ourselves in the proper environment of the blood and the atmosphere for several functions in the name of Jesus. We thank you that the blood of Jesus is an agent of purification. It is its own blood supply. It is our security agency. It is our emergency first aid kit and so we overcome by

the blood of Jesus Christ. We immerse ourselves in the blood of Jesus Christ.

We saturate our spirit, our consciousness, our discernment, our intuition, and our worship. We bathe our soul, our conscious, our subconscious, and unconscious mind, our will, our emotions, and our intellect. We soak our five senses in the blood of Jesus, our sight, our hearing, our smell, taste, and our touch. We submerge our physical bodies, our brain, our physical appetites, and our sexual character in the blood of Jesus. We throw buckets and buckets of blood, the blood of Jesus Christ and we boldly accept, multiplied grace and multiplied peace in the name of Jesus. We cover doorposts and our possessions. Those we love and those that love us with the blood of Jesus, we are made perfect through the blood of Jesus and his everlasting covenant. We have boldness and get dread to the presence of the Lord God for the blood of Jesus Christ. Our consciousness is purged from dead works through the blood of Jesus and we now serve a living God through the blood of Jesus.

We eat the body of Christ and we drink the blood of Jesus. According to John 6:54, we are redeemed through the blood of Jesus and we are rescued from the power of evil through the blood of Jesus. We release the power of the blood. We rebuke and cast out all spirits of torment and fear because we have peace through the blood of Jesus. We rebuke and cast out all spirits of guilt, shame, condemnation through the blood of Jesus. We rebuke Satan, the accuser of the brethren, and we remind him that he is a defeated foe through the blood of the Lord Jesus Christ. We receive the benefits of the new covenant through the blood of our savior Jesus Christ. We receive the healing, health and wealth through the blood of Jesus Christ. We receive abundance and prosperity, through the blood of Jesus Christ. We receive deliverance through the blood of Jesus Christ.

We receive the fullness of the Holy Ghost and the anointing through the blood of Jesus Christ. The blood of Jesus Christ bears witness to our deliverance and our salvation. The blood of Jesus Christ cleanses us from all unrighteousness and from all sin. Jesus Christ resisted unto death and his blood now gives us the victory. We destroy the power of sin, iniquity, and transgressions in our lives through the blood of Jesus. Our hearts have been covered with the blood of Jesus. Oh God, we thank you God, for the way I've been from an evil conscience. We release the blood of Jesus. We command all of our accusers to depart now through the blood of Jesus. We rebuke and cast out all spirits of slander and accusations through the blood of Jesus. We blind the eyes of all watcher spirits and all scanner spirits now in the name of Jesus and we cast on all spirits that will come to accuse, to slander, to destroy, to annihilate, to stop the movement of God in our lives with the blood of Jesus. We release the voice of the blood, against demons and evil spirits

that would accuse and condemn us in the name of Jesus, and we released the blood that is our intercessor to fight for us and to stand between life and death and to make sure that life is secure, in the Name of Jesus. We plead the blood of Jesus and we release the power of Jesus to begin to fight for us now, in Jesus' name.

You must apply the blood of Jesus when you're going into warfare. I think one of the things we don't really realize is that the blood of Jesus really is an **intercessor**. **It is also a warrior.** It really does speak for us. It covers us and protects us. We don't apply the blood of Jesus enough anymore in the church. We don't talk about the blood of Jesus or its eternal power enough. Therefore, when you're going into warfare, we must apply the **blood of Jesus.**

***

PRAYER SEQUENCE:

ADORATION

Daniel 2:20
and said: "Praise be to the name of God for ever and ever; wisdom and power are his.

Jeremiah 2:30
Sing to the LORD! Give praise to the LORD! He rescues the life of the needy from the hands of the wicked.

The LORD reigns, let the nations tremble; he sits enthroned between the cherubim, let the earth shake. ***2*** *Great is the LORD in Zion; he is exalted over*

all the nations. ***3*** *Let them praise your great and awesome name— he is*
holy. ***4*** *The King is mighty, he loves justice— you have established equity; in*
Jacob you have done what is just and right. ***5*** *Exalt the LORD our God and*
worship at his footstool; he is holy. ***6*** *Moses and Aaron were among his priests,*
Samuel was among those who called on his name; they called on the LORD and
he answered them. ***7*** *He spoke to them from the pillar of cloud; they kept his*
statutes and the decrees he gave them. ***8*** *LORD our God, you answered them;*
you were to Israel a forgiving God, though you punished their misdeeds. ***9*** *Exalt*
the LORD our God and worship at his holy mountain, for the LORD our God
is holy.

AFFIRMATION

John 3:3
I can see the Kingdom of God because I am born again.

Matthew 6:25-33
I don't worry about everyday life. God knows my needs and meets them because I make His Kingdom my primary concern.

John 14:21
Jesus shows himself to me because I love him.

Romans 5:10
Because Jesus died for my sins, I am no longer separated from God. I live in close union with him.

John 15:8
The fruit I produce brings great joy to God, my Father in Heaven.

2 Corinthians 12:9
God's power works best in my weakness.

Colossians 1:29
Through the energy of Christ working powerfully in me, I teach others His truths.

Ephesians 2:9-10
I have been saved, not by works, but grace, so that I might do good works.

Mark 5:34
My faith makes me whole in spirit, soul and body.

Jeremiah 33:3
When I call out to God He answers me. He tells me things I wouldn't know otherwise.

Isaiah 40:31
Because I place my hope in the Lord my strength is renewed.
Luke 24:36
As I follow Jesus – as I walk with him, I have peace.

John 15:10
Because I obey Jesus I remain in his love.

1 Corinthians 1:17
The cross of Christ is my power.

Philippians 4:19
My God meets all my needs.

Psalm 46:1
God is my refuge and strength; always ready to help me in times of trouble.

APPLY THE BLOOD

Hebrews 10:19
I have boldness to enter the presence of God through the Blood of Jesus Christ

Hebrews 13:20-21
I am made perfect through the Blood of the Everlasting Covenant

Hebrews 9:14
My conscience is purged from dead works to serve the living God through the Blood of Jesus Christ

CHAPTER 5

R – REPENTANCE, RECONCILIATION, & REDRESS

The next place we go to is **R** for **REPENTANCE.** Here where you go in and deal with your issues. We all live in this fallen world and as we walk through life, things will happen. **But you're still a warrior.** You're still a warrior. You've still got a battle to fight. You've still got a war to win. The Bible says that Jesus delights in dispensing mercy **(Micah 7:18)**. God delights in forgiving you. Therefore, don't sit in condemnation when you know that your family is on the line. When you know your family is at risk, when you know that your health is at risk, or when you know that you've got a death sentence over your head. The Bible says that you are to agree with your adversary quickly. Go before the Lord and you simply say, "Lord, forgive me, purge me, and wash me."

David did it in Psalm 51, in Psalm 38, and 18. It says, *I told you my sins and I am sorry for them.* It's simple. I told you my sins, God and I'm sorry for them. We have to learn how to **repent.** Then after we repent and ask God for forgiveness, we must move into **reconciliation.** We have to be reconciled back with our Father because nothing separates you from your power and from your authority and from your God like sin. Sometimes, the Holy Spirit has to remind you *exactly* what sin is because many love "loopholes." **Loopholes are an ambiguity or inadequacy in the law or a set of rules, which people can extort or manipulate for their advantage.** But can I tell you something? God is either right or He is wrong. He's either black or He is white. There are no gray areas with God. You're either holy or you're dirty. You're either righteous or you're wrong. Therefore, the gift repentance allows is for us to get back in right standing with God. **We cannot miss this step.**

We give the enemy access to our authority when we don't cleanse ourselves of **unrighteousness.**

Here's why: The Bible says that Satan has the authority to go before God and blaspheme your God when you sin. Now, I don't know about you, but I cried for two days when I realized that. When I do something wrong, when I sin, it gives Satan the capacity, the authority, and all of the ammunition that he needs to go into the courtrooms of my God call Him a liar. Because I said I believed in Him, but I did something totally opposite. Because I said that I was a Son of God, but I acted like I was Lucifer's best friend instead.

We give the enemy access to our authority when we don't cleanse ourselves of **unrighteousness.** It gives the enemy the right to stand in front of **your** God curse Him. It also gives the enemy the right to accuse you. He says: just look at what your children are doing. We must get repentance right and then we have to be reconciled back to God. It's so easy, but we make it so hard.

When I would travel to Brazil, we would go to the giant statue of Jesus in Rio de Janeiro. There, you could see people taking those 300 steps on their knees as penance for sin and I would just walk right past them and say "the blood of Jesus" as I passed. I didn't have to do all of that. Thank God I don't have to do all of that. The blood of Jesus already made a way of escape for me.

The Redress

David said listen, wash me and cleanse me. As David demonstrated, we need to be reconciled to God and then **redressed** (to remedy or set right an undesirable or unfair situation). Often, we must get rid of sin because somewhere we removed our armor. (knowingly or unknowingly). The Bible instructs us to put on the WHOLE armor of God and this is how we can stand against the enemy. If the enemy is encroaching, then you're likely having demonic interference, or you need some type of deliverance. When this occurs, there's at least one piece of your armor you have taken off for one reason or the other. Can I tell you that most of the time it's the **belt of truth?**

The belt of truth covers up the sacred parts of you. Either we don't walk in our truth or we let people in the cookie jar that's not our mate. We don't belong to them and they don't belong to us. It's under that belt of truth that we tend to get in the most trouble. But if we can just understand that this area is the most sacred area on your body, besides your heart. Specifically, to women, if we can just understand that the womb is an **incubator** for so many things. This is the most sacred part of who you are and when you take that belt off, disease comes, death comes, generational curses come – just to name a few. Why? Because God said, I'm going to put a seed in here and that seed is going to hate the devil if you teach it right. If you raise that child right, that child will become an enemy of Satan. Then He said that *your seed will bruise the head of the serpent.* If you train up that child correctly, that child will love what God loves and hate what God hates. If you train at child right, when they do wrong, something inside of them will tether them and pull them back. This is the most sacred part of who you are. There is an egg in there—something waiting to be birthed both in the natural and in the spiritual, right there in your womb.

So, you've got to go back and redress that area. You've got to put truth back in its place. You've got to walk with the word of God. You got to tell the truth about where you are and what happened, what you wanted to do, what you're fighting trying not to do, and what you're trying to come out of. The Bible says that it's the truth that makes us free **(John 8:32).** Why do we think we can hide from God? God wants you to redress. He wants you to put your armor back on and stand against the wiles of the enemy.

You do realize that there's no armor for the backside? The reason that there is no armor for the backside is because you don't need it. There's a lion that roars behind you. **There's a King that backs what you say.** There are angels that back what you say. You don't need any armor on your backside because if God is for you, who can be against you **(Romans 8:31)?**

We MUST remember to redress.

CHAPTER 6

M – MEDITATE ON THE WORD OF GOD

Now we must meditate on the word of God. One of the things I teach at my church is when you're preparing to pray openly (before a service), I instruct them to listen to what the Holy Ghost wants you to pray for or what your leaders have assigned you to pray. Don't just pray without structure; haphazardly. Understand what the assignment is for that moment and release it through prayer. Find scriptures on the topic or scriptures related to the specific prayer assignment. Find at least five scriptures that coincide with what you have been tasked with praying about. If you pray God's word back to Him, He will respond.

For instance: *The word of God declares that we overcome by the blood of the lamb and the word of our testimony* **(Revelation 12:11)** and so the way we can incorporate this scripture into our prayer like this: Father, I apply the blood of Jesus to my life, and to my testimony. One time, I heard a woman in service very simply give her testimony, that's all she did—**and it was powerful.**

Any time we engage in prayer of any kind, the most effective tool we have at our disposal is the Word of God. Any intercessor that desires meaningful spiritual growth and mastery of their craft must become students of the Holy Word of God. It is imperative that we are accurate from a biblical perspective in order to gain the victory we are promised when we pray. In the Word of God, we can see how Jehoshaphat used his knowledge of what the Lord had done in times past in order to gather his strength for battle.

5 *Then Jehoshaphat stood up in the assembly of Judah and Jerusalem at the temple of the LORD in the front of the new courtyard*

6 *and said: "LORD, the God of our ancestors,* ***are you not*** *the God who is in heaven? You rule over all the kingdoms of the nations. Power and might are in your hand, and no one can withstand you.*

7 *Our God,* ***did you not*** *drive out the inhabitants of this land before your people Israel and give it forever to the descendants of Abraham your friend?*

8 They have lived in it and have built in it a sanctuary for your Name, saying,

9 'If calamity comes upon us, whether the sword of judgment, or plague or famine, we will stand in your presence before this temple that bears your Name and will cry out to you in our distress, and you will hear us and save us.'

10 "But now here are men from Ammon, Moab and Mount Seir, whose territory you would not allow Israel to invade when they came from Egypt; so, they turned away from them and did not destroy them.

11 See how they are repaying us by coming to drive us out of the possession you gave us as an inheritance.

12 Our God, will you not judge them? For we have no power to face this vast army that is attacking us. We do not know what to do, but our eyes are on you."

13 All the men of Judah, with their wives and children and little ones, stood there before the LORD."

In this passage we see that Jehoshaphat begins to recall the history of God's mighty hand to protect and save his people. There were no

A skillful warrior always fights from the commands of God.

published Bibles at that time, but they kept the deeds alive in their hearts, in holy assemblies, through the priesthood, and in their prayers to God. Living in this modern age of technology, we must also access God's history and triumphant victories. We can search for the scriptures that will strengthen and guide us through the battles we will face during times of spiritual warfare.

A skillful warrior always fights from the commands of God. We must be commissioned not only through The Spirit of God but also through The Word of God. Anytime you feel the call to intercede it is important to go to The Word of God to secure scriptural weapons to add to your arsenal. The enemy is very bold and violent, but he cannot stand against the Word of God. The Word of God is an effective tool when entering into any kind of prayer, but it is most effective in warfare. Why? Because God responds to His Word concerning matters that he is concerned about. God always shows up where His Word is. God and The Word of God are one (John 1:1). Using the Word of God is the most effective way to ensure victory. The Word of God is a weapon of mass destruction when used in its proper context. The Word promises that He and His Word will go with us in battle **(Exodus 14:14).**

The LORD Himself goes before you; He will be with you. He will never leave you nor forsake you. Do not be afraid or discouraged. Deuteronomy 31:8

****

Let's see how God responded to Jehshaphat:

14 Then the Spirit of the LORD came on Jahaziel son of Zechariah, the son of Benaiah, the son of Jeiel, the son of Mattaniah, a Levite and descendant of Asaph, as he stood in the assembly.

15 He said: "Listen, King Jehoshaphat and all who live in Judah and Jerusalem! This is what the LORD says to you: 'Do not be afraid or discouraged because of this vast army. For the battle is not yours, but God's.

16 Tomorrow march down against them. They will be climbing up by the Pass of Ziz, and you will find them at the end of the gorge in the Desert of Jeruel.

17 You will not have to fight this battle. Take up your positions; stand firm and see the deliverance the LORD will give you, Judah and Jerusalem. Do not be afraid; do not be discouraged. Go out to face them tomorrow, and the LORD will be with you."

18 Jehoshaphat bowed down with his face to the ground, and all the people of Judah and Jerusalem fell down in worship before the LORD.

19 Then some Levites from the Kohathites and Korahites stood up and praised the LORD, the God of Israel, with a very loud voice.

20 Early in the morning they left for the Desert of Tekoa. As they set out, Jehoshaphat stood and said, "Listen to me, Judah and people of Jerusalem! Have faith in the LORD your God and you will be upheld; have faith in his prophets and you will be successful."

21 After consulting the people, Jehoshaphat appointed men to sing to the LORD and to praise him for the splendor of his holiness as they went out at the head of the army, saying: "Give thanks to the LORD, for his love endures forever."

22 *As they began to sing and praise, the LORD set ambushes against the men of Ammon and Moab and Mount Seir who were invading Judah, and they were defeated."*

Jehoshaphat used what he knew about God according to the history of his people with God to encourage himself and to get God to engage in battle with him. We cannot lose when we use the scriptures as a weapon.

We must remember to use the word in all aspects of Spiritual warfare and intercession.

Prepare For Battle

As I began to seek the Lord for strategy, he took me to a very interesting passage of scripture:

"Then he took his staff in his hand, chose five smooth stones from the stream, put them in the pouch of his shepherd's bag and, with his sling in his hand, approached the Philistine." 1 Samuel 17:40

We know that Saul had previously offered his armor to David, but David declined saying that "he was not accustomed to them." **(1 Samuel 17:39)** This scripture holds so much meat for the intercessor. It tells us that we each wear and use different weaponry. Every intercessor must first be a student of the Word of God. You must be proficient in rightly dividing scripture and using them in a context that is appropriate for the kind of prayers the situation calls for. My purpose for writing this book is not only to provide a new model for prayer but to also remind the intercessor that the weapon of the word is our strongest ally. So just as David picked up five smooth stones, we must approach the duties of prayer by selecting appropriate scriptures that lead to our victory in battle.

5 Smooth Stones = 5 Smooth Scriptures

Whenever we begin to prepare for prayer, we must attack it with scriptures. The word of God must be the first tool that we pick up when preparing for intercession. After the burden of the Lord comes upon us to pray, we must immediately seek the appropriate scriptures. I recommend during your time of preparation (yes, you must prepare before you pray) gather no fewer than **five scriptures** to assist you in your attack.

Scriptures help to target certain prayer points. We must select appropriate scriptures that promise of a victorious outcome and meditate on those scriptures. Allow those scriptures to sink into your spirit. Allow them to become a part of your cadence for war. Meditating on the Word of the Lord and then using them when hitting your target pushes the enemy like no other weapon can. Meditating on scripture builds your confidence to pray boldly. It equips you with strength, courage, and confidence that our God will do what the scriptures say he has done, is doing, and **WILL DO FOR YOU!**

Whenever we are assigned to war against something, we must find appropriate scriptures. If we are praying against something, we must remember to find scriptures that are applicable to what it is we are praying against or for and we must pray those scriptures. We must declare and we decree from the word of God and declare what God says about that matter. Sometimes your faith may be shaky. Sometimes you think the issue, the problem, or the assignment is so big that you may not think God can really perform it. You need the word of God to encourage you because God is not a liar and He doesn't live in doubt. In fact, if you read your Bible, **Revelation 21:8** says that of all the people that will go to hell, those of us who had no faith in God will also go. Read your Bible. If more people were aware of this scripture and really understood its meaning, then many wouldn't have the mindset of "once saved, always saved." The Bible is very clear. If you have no faith, you will go to hell just like sorcerers, like murderers, and like liars - just like these people, you'll go to hell as well.

Why? Faith is the currency of heaven. Therefore, if you don't have an exchange, how can you enter? So, there you are raising your hand in church, but in your heart, you actually doubt God. You've got to read your Bible because some of these "revelations" that people are teaching are nothing more than trends. It is a "trend" when you believe it but it has no biblical foundation. I visited a church once and they became angry at me because I told them they should have told me what they were teaching on and I would I told you that I wasn't coming. I told them that I'm going to walk you through the scriptures because what's being taught is not what the Bible says. I know I'm wrecking some people right now, but you need to be wrecked. But if you don't build your faith in order to fight, how can God say to you, well done?

If you miss your assignment, how at the end of your life can God say to you, well done "thy good and faithful servant" when you've never served him? You've served the church, you've served your pastor, you've served your auxiliary, but you've never served God? Make sure you have scripture and never go into prayer without God's word. Be sure to meditate on it and let it get into your bones. Think about it. **Research it. Study it.** If there's a word that jumps out to you, look for the definition of that word. Just don't move past it quickly. Study it! Make sure you understand what is in God's original script.

Study your word to make sure you're hitting your target. The Bible says we pray amiss **(James 4:3).** That means when we're not educated and intelligent when it comes to prayer, we may miss our target(s). You must be intelligent when you pray. I can appreciate the moans and the groans, but God gave you words to assault the enemy with. He gave you a sound that frightens the enemy and pushes him back - he gave you intelligence. The Apostle Paul said, "I pray that you have wisdom, revelation, and knowledge **(Ephesians 1:17).**

That's the Apostolic prayer Paul prayed. That you would walk in wisdom, revelation, and knowledge. Stop being so mesmerized because somebody took the time to get a revelation that you didn't. You've got to have your own revelation. Quite often, others don't always have the time to go into your situation, but you do! Let God reveal the root of the problem to you. Let God reveal the heart of the matter to you. Let God reveal himself to you.

We must meditate on God's word and use the word of God during prayer. I love prayer so much. People usually don't invite me to pray most times because when I get started, I get going! As a matter of fact, just don't even invite me for Thanksgiving dinner to pray! I understand that it is communication with God, and I get to talk to my daddy. I get to talk to my commander-in-chief, and I am able to legislate on his behalf, but I can't do it if I don't know what he's saying. Therefore, just like David had five smooth stones, make sure you have five "smooth" scriptures that will knock the enemy's head clean off. Five smooth scriptures will prove to you that you're supposed to be healed, that you're supposed to be whole, and that you're supposed to be perfect. Five smooth scriptures before you pray. **Put some WORD on it!**

PRAYER SEQUENCE:

MEDITATE ON THE WORD OF GOD

Incorporate the word of God during prayer in order to hit a specific target within the enemy's camp.

The word you study and pray gives you a **focus point.**

What does the Holy Spirit want you to specifically attack in prayer?

Once he answers, find at least **5 scriptures.** Take those scriptures and study them. Use them as a map to attack the assignment at hand.

We must consistently be:

- **Intelligent**
- **Knowledgeable**
- **Teachable**

We must flow together.

Studying the scriptures remove pride from your prayer time.

It reduces the chances that we pray and MISS THE TARGET!

Too many pray out of routine, ritual, and just plain pride. But people in the foxhole with you get injured when we do.

THE WORD WILL COVER YOU IN PRAYER. YOUR WORDS HAVE NO POWER RXCEPT THEY COME FROM GOD'S RULES OF ENGAGEMENT.
USE THE WORD!

CHAPTER 7

E - EMPLOY & ENGAGE

Now, here is when we employ our angels. We know of the angels in the Bible - we know Michael, we know Gabriel, but often we don't realize that God **has an entire army.** He has legions and legions of angels and there are legions of angels whose sole job it is to fight for **you**. Their only job is to back what you say and stand there and tell the enemy: **I WISH YOU WOULD!** Their sole job is to bring healing to your bones so that you can get back in the warfare. Their sole job is to make sure you fulfill your purpose, but if you've never engaged them how can they do their job? This is the place where God gave me a greater understanding of the purpose of angels. One day as was praying **Psalm 91** and I focused in on the part where it talks about "those who abide in the shadow" of the almighty. This day I had been going forth and engaging in prayer and then He said,

"Now back up." I said, "huh?" He said, "Now back up, under my wing, under my shadow." So, I backed up. He said, "Now tell them (the angels) what to do. You no longer must fight. USE YOUR ANGELS! That's what they are there for!" Many times, we have casualties-of-war because we are standing in the front with all our pride. GET OUT OF THE WAY! Let angels do what they're assigned to do.

Who are Angels?

Angels are one of the most underused accompaniments from God given to help us achieve victory over the kingdom of darkness. As a soldier in the Lord's Army, you are actively involved in the kingdom ministry of bringing healing and freedom to suffering nations, regions, and souls. In the pursuit of victory, you will most certainly end up on the radar of our enemy, Satan and his fallen legion of angels. Sadly, very few teach the essential prayers of authoritative warfare that are necessary to protect nations, families, and individuals from the retaliatory onslaught of a "kingdom" that has set its sights on killing, stealing, and destroying our efforts to build and advance the kingdom of our God. For this reason, God has given us angels to use for our defense.

In addition to our Jesus-given authority, we have been given the assistance of holy angels who are deployed for the purpose of aiding us in our time of warfare.

I remember the first time I encountered an angel. My husband and I just came out of a hard season in our marriage. My husband lived in two different cities for a little over a year. One day my pastor at the time gave me the instruction to return home to my husband because God had promised to heal us and protect our union. Out of obedience I went back home. In anticipation of my homecoming, my husband prepared a new home for our family. In obedience to the counsel of my trusted pastor, my son and I went back home to join my husband.

We'd settle into our new home and reignited our love for each other. One day, as I was climbing the steps of our home headed towards our beautiful bedroom when suddenly, I heard someone laughing a very sinister laugh. As I reached the doorway of our bedroom, I was caught up in a vision of a demon laughing and telling me that my marriage would never work because he would destroy it. The demon was laughing so hard and so loud that it startled me. Seeing spirits was something I was accustomed to even as a child. The unseen realm had always been as real to me as my visible world. As a young, unsaved child I would see spirits walking among us and was often terrified by them. Now that I'd given my life over to Christ, I was now more comfortable with seeing spirits even though I wasn't being taught much more than "the devil was busy" in church. However, I stood there and gazed at this demon sitting on a thrown taunting me and telling me his plans to destroy my marriage. In an instant, a huge presence entered the room. This being was so large that only the legs and part of the torso could be seen. At first, I was startled because I was unable to determine whether this evil spirit had summoned other demon spirits or if God had come to rescue me. The air in the room grew quiet. There was no movement, no wind, and no sound. Then, I could see that this "being" was an angel—a very large angel who'd stepped into the room to defeat this demon and to assure me that my marriage was safe. The angel stretched out his glorious wings and they covered the entire perimeter of the room. I could see the torso of this being. It was strong and well equipped with an arsenal of heavenly weapons. He destroyed the demonic presence that had been taunting me with one swift move. **I was free.** That angel then took those same wings and wrapped me under his protection, and I knew the battle was over and I was safe.

I understood then that ANGELS ARE AT OUR DISPOSAL and ready to be deployed in order to protect what God has ordained. After that encounter, I was no longer afraid of what I saw in the unseen realm because I knew I had an angel – an ally in the battles that I was ordained to fight.

How Do Angels Work?

Angels work diligently to **protect**, **heal**, **encourage**, and **strengthen** believers. They too are a part of the armies that God engages and sanctions for warfare. We are never fighting alone! Some of the most epic battles in the Bible are those where the angels come to the aid of God's children to **ensure victory**. In today's climate, demonic activity is on the rise. Demons are real. They are formidable enemies who work tirelessly to cause God's kingdom to be diminished. According to **Revelation 12:12**, Satan is increasing his activity because he knows his time is short. We are seeing so much demonic activity because he has a limited time to be in possession of a fallen world. Our job is to war in conjunction with our angels to ensure that the kingdom of darkness does not advance. Angels aid us in launching powerful counterattacks. Angels work tirelessly to ensure that we, the joint heirs of Jesus Christ, overcome the plots, plans, and schemes of the evil one.

➢ **Angels <u>work together</u> with us in our service for God.**

"This is the same Moses whom they earlier rejected, saying, 'Who put you in charge of us?' This is the Moses that God, using the angel flaming in the burning bush, sent back as ruler and redeemer. Acts 7:35

➢ **Angels <u>bring deliverance</u> from enemy hands.**

"But during the night an angel of the Lord opened the doors of the jail and brought them out." Acts 5:19

➢ **God's angels <u>fight against</u> the angels of Satan.**

Then he continued, Do not be afraid, Daniel. Since the first day that you set your mind to gain understanding and to humble yourself before your God, your words were heard, and I have come in response to them.

But the prince of the Persian kingdom resisted me twenty-one days. Then Michael, one of the chief princes, came to help me, because I was detained there with the king of Persia. Daniel 10:12-13

I was so excited when I finally discovered the truth about spiritual warfare: We do not fight against the *princes*—the fallen angels, we exercise our authority over demons. However, we also influence the "warring angels" assigned to fight on our behalf when we pray to God!

Command your angels. Tell them what to do, where to go, and what to fight. When Daniel knew that the 70 years of enslavement was over, he prayed and never moved from his position. For 21 days, there was a war in heaven. Michael was fighting with the principality, the Prince over Persia for 21 days but Daniel never moved from his seated position. He never moved from being under the shadow of the almighty. He never moved from his place of prayer. He didn't get up to try and help God in any way. HE NEVER MOVED! **He used the angels.**

You must use your help. For those of you who have never heard about the ministry of angels, make sure to study it for yourself. If you're hearing something new, don't take my word for it. The Bible says that he loved the Bereans. Why? They studied the word of God. Therefore, it is from this hidden position where we now engage in warfare. We are guilty of having too many casualties of war—intercessors who don't know how to apply the blood, how to put on the armor, or how to step back and let angels take care of what they're in charge of. Do you know that there are wars in the heavenlies day and night concerning you and your purpose?

Jesus is always interceding for you. Some of the casualties we go through, we don't have to. Then sometimes we have needless casualties because we're just repeating stuff that other people have authority over, but we don't. I know this is strong but let me tell you something: until you've been through "some" guerrilla-warfare training in the spirit, you'd better stay with Jesus loves the little children! **Let God help you to understand your rank.** In the traditional military, guerrilla warfare is a form of irregular warfare in which small groups of combatants, such as paramilitary personnel, armed civilians, or irregulars, use military tactics including ambushes, sabotage, raids, petty warfare, hit-and-run tactics, and mobility, to fight a larger and less-mobile, traditional military.

There's a war for foot soldiers just like there are wars for generals. **There's still something for you to do.** No matter what your rank is, whether you're a general, a Sergeant, a Colonel, a major, a Drill Sergeant, a First Sergeant, a Sergeant major. No matter what you are, or a private. The moment you get saved, you can engage in warfare, cover yourself with the blood of Jesus and go at it. There's a rank for everybody but you've got to be responsible and be intentional about understanding what your rank is.

Know Your Rank, Your Responsibility and Your Requirements in Warfare

Once, God sent me to a particular region on an assignment from Heaven. While there, I was taken up in a dream and given a battle matrix and plan for this particular assignment. God downloaded His battle plan to me which included a very strategic plan to expose and war against the princes of that region. I disseminated this intel to the apostles and leaders for that region who were in attendance that morning. After reviewing, confirming, and discussing that intel, I was asked to lead them in a sequence of strong prayer and spiritual warfare. We were dealing with a strong prince and the assignment demanded the apostolic authority of the leaders in that region. This prayer needed to be executed in unity and amongst the apostolic figures in that region. We gathered, repented, covered ourselves properly, and I led them in prayer.

After we competed the sequence a young lady from the service approached me and she asked if she could have a copy of the prayer? I looked at her, I said, "no ma'am." She said, "why not?" I said, "because the Lord said I couldn't give it to you. You're not ready." We continued to have a dialogue about the prayer assignment God had issued for the leaders and what had transpired with the leaders previously.

Many times, we can "hear" someone pray and because we don't realize the weight of their words and assignment, we believe we can just repeat what they've prayed. Often times, we like to repeat a lot of prayers because it sounds good and it sounds powerful, but until you know that you are powerful enough to back up every word you say, it helps to add value to your prayer assignment. It's like giving you a missile and you don't know how to activate the sequence code. We must remember that the enemy has weapons as well and we must be **properly prepared**. We must understand where we fit in the Lord's army in order to wage a good warfare—and have success.

Remember, the enemy has a missile pointed at you too. Therefore, we must be careful and we must remember to war where you are. Be effective where you are and don't try to come out of your grace before your time or what you've been prepared for. Intercession is a vital part of spiritual warfare. We all have a place, a part, and an assignment. We need warfare at every level. God has a specific assignment for every believer. The Bible says the kingdoms

There is a place, a grace, and assignment for everyone.

of this world should become the Kings of his Lord and of his Christ. In order to topple kingdoms, we need troops on every level in order to strike an effective blow. **There is a place, a grace, and an assignment for everyone.**

In order to master your battlefield, it is imperative to know your assignment and to matriculate through your assigned ranks. **Heaven has use of you right where you are, for whatever the season in you are in.** For example: your assignment may be to pray for children. In order to be promoted or given a higher level of insight or heavenly intel, you will need to be diligent as a foot soldier executing your proper due diligence with God and with your strategic mapping and study—right there. Before entering prayer, you will need some reconnaissance. A **reconnaissance mission** is defined as the act of observing, especially to gain information about an enemy or potential enemy.

Effective intercession and warfare begin with elements of **worship, study, and discernment**. We must begin with a study of what God wants for the children and what's opposing the children in your region. Look at the statistics of children that are born to unwed mothers or the number of dropouts occurring concerning teenagers. Investigate the crime stats. What kinds of crimes are teens under the age of 18 committing? **Pray against that**. What are the entry points? What are the main, opposing factors? What is the intended plan of God for the children you are assigned to? Are there curses or any legal rights that would give access to the enemy that must be dealt with? Next, how do you begin to tackle this assignment? Once you have answered these questions, then you are ready to enter into the *Battle Matrix* with the proper weapons and information. Now, you can pray against molestation. Pray against incest, pray against sex-trafficking. Pray against those things that oppose children.

We always desire the blessings of God for our assigned prayer targets; however, **God can't truly bless it until he cleans it.** We are skipping the cleaning part and going straight to the blessing. For instance, at my house, I don't cook anything until I bleach it. So, you've got to get rid of those things that are tormenting children. **You've got to engage in warfare for them.**

PRAYER SEQUENCE:

ENGAGE IN WARFARE

Now that you have prepared yourself using:

- The Blood of Jesus
- Angels
- The whole armor of God
- Seated in heavenly places

Here is where we hide ourselves under the shadow of the ALMIGHTY and command the angelic soldiers to take over!

Now we: can:

- Decree victory!
- Declare that if God be for us who can be against us?
- Boldly declare that the Kingdoms of this world shall be the Kingdom of our God.

CHAPTER 8

D - DESTROY THE WORKS OF THE DEVIL

The enemy is **deceptive**, **divisive**, **devouring**, and **dark**. Satan's character is dark because he is completely, and eternally, **severed** from God's everlasting Light **(Matthew 6:23). God is the source of all life.** The devil, by his very nature, as being eternally severed from God, destroys life. Therefore, we must keep the darkness from devouring the world we live in. **1 Peter 5:8-9** describes the enemy as *walking about like a roaring lion.* Lions do not kill indiscriminately, nor merely because it's just his nature; but lions only kill when it suits his purpose and when he thinks he has a reasonable chance of success with minimal resistance. No one blames a lion for killing. Because it is the nature of a lion to strike the prey that exhibits the least amount of resistance, **ENGAGING IN WARFARE IS A MUST.** We must give the enemy a good fight, not only that we destroy his plots, schemes, traps, and snares. The devil was the first to prefer choice rather than life and he has been preaching the same message ever since. We must destroy his deception and free ourselves from his grip entirely. *The coming of the lawless one is according to the working of Satan, with all power, signs, and lying wonders, and with all unrighteous deception among those who perish, because they did not receive the love of the truth, that they might be saved,* 2 **Thessalonians 2:9-10**. We must take every measure available to protect the family of God by destroying the intended plans of the enemy. WE MUST DESTROY HIS WORKS.

Satan's mission is to dethrone God, destroy all of creation, deceive the world (if possible, even the very elect) divide the world, and especially the Church. Our mission is salvation, illumination, sanctification, and reconciliation. Our mission also includes destroying his works and bringing captive kingdoms back to God. Our Commander-and-Chief has provided us with everything we need for victory on the battlefield at His own expense. He has promised us eternal life even if our mortal body is destroyed. He has promised and is faithful to provide victory in this life and beyond.

"...I now send you, to open their eyes, in order to turn them from darkness to light, and from the power of Satan to God, that they may receive forgiveness of sins and an inheritance among those who are sanctified by faith in Me." ***Acts 26:17-18***

"Now all things are of God, who has reconciled us to Himself through Jesus Christ, and has given us the ministry of reconciliation..." **2 Corinthians 5:18-20**

~

Now, you have prepared yourself, you have used the blood of Jesus, you have dispatched angels, you have put on the whole armor of God, and now you're seated in heavenly places. Here is where we hide under the shadow of the almighty and command the angelic soldiers to take over. Now, we can decree. Now, we can declare. Now, we can take territory. Now we can see movement. Now, we can see God taking over at this place and finally destroying the works of the devil. This is your assignment. **In Luke 9:10**, he deputized (the process of empowering someone who is to act as a substitute for his superior) you to cast out devils and to heal the sick. He says, we don't wrestle against flesh and blood; however, there is a wrestling match for all of us and we must wrestle in prayer. This means that we have got to get up close and personal. When this happens, whatever you are praying against just may hit your house only so you can learn how to wrestle with it and thereby, learn how to defeat it.

Deputized: the process of empowering someone to act as substitute for their superior.

Get My Stuff Also

When a newcomer enters into military, the focus is usually on the individual. As he/she enters basic training, the focus changes to the soldier's efforts at becoming a member of the battalion or troop. At this point, the "me" is now turned upside-down and is transformed into "we". From the moment they report for duty to the day they leave the service, their life is defined by one word: **mission**. We must all answer the call to Kingdom service. Intercessors must never get past the fact that the world doesn't revolve around them, their dreams, their goals, their desires, or their personal needs. We must grasp the concept that everything we do reflects upon and effects the kingdom: the family, the church, and Jesus Christ. As intercessors, our process is the same is the same as soldiers. I believe that intercessors function best in teams or troops. **Troops help to combat individuality in order to adhere to an overall mission, and to answer the call to serve God with others in order to create an army against the armies of Satan.**

We must always remember that every battle has a more crucial war. There are constant battles in the heavenly places that affect the climate and culture of the world we live in. The enemy lives in constant opposition of God, always exemplifying the contrarian that is against every idea except his own. **Intercessors must keep this in mind when praying for a specific person or situation**.

Perhaps your child or a precious soul is battling an addiction and may take a little detour into drugs. We must remember that our prayer assignments are always attached to a bigger war on the spiritual battleground. When Jesus carried His cross to Calvary and died, that wasn't for him; it was for all of mankind. While you are laboring in prayer to "snatch" that person from the grasp of the enemy, you (*the Church* and intercessors) act, move, and engage solely in Christ's name. We do not wage war in any other name or under any other mission.

Some warriors are simply lying down. You have suffered battle fatigue (A stress syndrome, now usually called post-traumatic stress disorder, caused by prolonged exposure to the trauma of warfare). I COMMAND YOU, to get up and fight the enemy back! You are *not* fighting alone. You have the authority to destroy the works of the devil. ***1 John 3:8*** *says, whoever makes a practice of sinning is of the devil.* For the devil has been sinning from the beginning.

You must understand that the VERY reason the Son of God appeared was to DESTROY THE WORKS OF THE DEVIL. He didn't just appear, but he said, I'm going to make you in my image and in my likeness. Everything that Jesus defeated, you have defeated. Everything that Jesus destroyed, you can destroy also.

Measure Effectiveness

The kingdom has landed, God has arrived, the general has taken command, and it is our mission to search and to destroy the works of the devil. Here is where you can document and measure victories. There was a time is our city that men were murdering their wives at an alarming rate. It's alarming because I affectionately call my home city Minivan Land. We began having a rash of spousal murders that was very uncommon for our region. One day the Holy Spirit commissioned me to pray. I gathered recent articles, I looked up demographics and statistics, found scripters to accompany my counter-attack, and spoke with the media rep for our sheriff's department. I asked God specifically how to pray and who to get to join me and we started praying. We began to pray against the spirit of murder and against other spirits that were robbing my community of its mothers. We prayed until we saw the numbers go down. If we saw police brutality, then we would pray until it stopped happening or until will saw certain laws legislated and initiatives implemented to foster better police and citizen collaboration.

We are in the midst of a national opioid crisis and the sheriff in my area called and asked me to pray. He informed me that they have had 13 children recently die from this current strain of heroin. Can you pray? When they posted pictures of our governor and he was in blackface, lawmakers convened at our state capital and they looked to me for prayer and strategy. They called and said, "Apostle, what should we do?"

<u>How We Measure Victory</u> –

- Get your target in focus.
- Conduct your preparation and mapping using a **Battle Matrix Journal.**
- Gather your troops.
- Make the assignment clear to them.
- Pray until Heaven responds.
- Look for the signs that the enemy has backed up; testimonies, newspaper articles, statistics, healings, and hearing from God that the mission was successful.

You will start to see the outcome(s). It'll be in the newspapers. It'll be on the news. You will hear people testifying in your church about certain breakthroughs they have received. You will see children who were once wayward come back to God. You will witness healings, deliverance, and salvation. **You can measure the success of your prayers when you target your prayers.**

<u>VICTORY – That's Our Battle Cry</u>

Here is where we see victory. So, once you begin to see victory, you're now in a "cooling off" period. Think about when you exercise very strenuously. After you're done working out, there's usually a cooling-off period. A time where the heart rate comes back down to normal and the muscles and joints also begin to normalize. It is at this moment; you go back to the angels and you declare and decree that there will be no retaliation for the work that you have done for the kingdom of God. You not only go back to the angels, but you also go back to the blood and declare that there will be no retaliation from the enemy. At the cooling-off period, we also go back to adoration. We worship again.

You must understand that though you have been armed for battle, you have also been equipped to be accurate in battle. You are a skull-crushing, bone-crushing warrior for God. The things that have been opposing you, it's time for YOU to **depose** them.

OUR CHALLENGE:

Let's go get our stuff back. Let's win. We're in a time now where people are saying that nothing is coming to pass. Most are used to receiving a word, but there are not experiencing fruit from that word. I want you to have fruit and I want you to pick a target. I want you to use the strategy.

Victory is inevitable.

PRAYER SEQUENCE:

DESTROY THE WORKS OF THE DEVIL

1 John 3:8

Whoever makes a practice of sinning is of the devil, for the devil has been sinning from the beginning. The reason the Son of God appeared was to destroy the works of the devil.

Here we can:

- Tear down altars
- Throw Jezebel down
- Overthrow satanic governments and systems

The reason the Son of God appeared was to destroy the works of the devil.

The kingdom has landed, the doctor has arrived, and the general has taken command! **Our mission: search and destroy the works of the devil.**

CHAPTER 9

WAKE UP! WAKE UP!

Wake up! Wake up, Deborah, Wake up! Wake up and break out in song! Arise, Barak, take captive your captains. The scripture is telling us that it is time for the kingdom to now WAKE UP! It's time for you to stop praying prayers that don't result in any movement. It's time to stop taking blows from the enemy. It's time to now get into an **offensive** position and instead of a **defensive** position. It's time. Satan is the accuser of the brethren and it's time for the sons of God to begin accusing him! It's time to call him a liar, to call him a defeated foe, to push him back and to remind him that he's already lost this war! **It's time for us to become ARMED.**

A NOTE TO WOMEN WHO WAR:

When the Bible talks about that he will make a suitable helper for a man. That word there is EZER and it's a military weapon. It's a military term. It means that you were created to be a military aid to a man. You are not supposed to be someone who is just satisfied with a penis and a pocketbook! You are supposed to be somebody who could turn his head and who could influence him in the direction of the King. You are the one who's supposed to turn him to God. You're the one that intercedes for him. You're the one that prays for him to make sure the enemy can't take him out. You are the one who is supposed to make sure his purpose is fulfilled. You're supposed to be a military aid to a man. You're not a damsel in distress. You are a dangerous daughter of the King.

You're not weak, you are a righteous rebel. God didn't make you weak. Some of you have birthed babies out of your bodies. You're not built to be weak. You have co-created life with God therefore, he has never made you weak. We must get into a posture where we can identify ourselves as daughters of God and we must take that authority by walking in the truth of who we are. Don't let anybody make you believe that being aggressive is a bad thing. Don't let anybody tell you that being direct is a bad thing. Don't let anyone convince you that being assertive is a bad thing. Deborah was assertive, she was aggressive, and she got the job done. She even had an assassin working with her on her team. Her name was Jael and the Bible considered her a heroine who killed Sisera to deliver Israel from the troops of King Jabin. Jael took the enemy out. She said, "Deborah if you can't get to it, I can! If you don't come into your tent, I DECLARE - that if he comes into my tent, he's gone!" Jael says, "I'm to going to use everything I have—all of my beauty, all of my seduction, I'm going to use everything to make sure Sisera comes into my tent!

I'm going to feed him, I'm going to let him lay his head down on my lap, and I'm going to drive that stake all the way through his skull! He's going to be gone by the time I'm finished!" That's who you are.

Don't let anyone tell you that you're too much. Don't let anyone convince you that you're too hard to deal with or you're too much to take. They're just not your people. But there are people who love the fact that you're direct, who loved the fact that you will go after something and you will kill it—in Jesus' name! Your people are people who love the fact that they can trust you to pray them through. Your people love the fact that you're going to get results when you open your mouth.

CHAPTER 10

THE ROLE OF THE INTERCESSOR IN SPIRITUAL WARFARE

I once read a pamphlet called ***The Cavalry Commander*** by Xenophon. This celebrated, historic manuscript is writing instructions to those who aspired to be an officer in the **Athenian Equestrian Corps**. As I read it, I began to see the duties and requirements of those who desired to become intercessors that God could both use and promote. The author gives a vivid outline of the duties that one must take on—not as suggestions, but as disciplines in order to excel. Here is my version of those duties from the perspective of one who is looking to raise up an army of intercessors who endeavor to achieve mastery intercession.

First Duty

The first duty of an intercessor is to offer sacrifices of worship and praise to God. Secondly, pray for Him to grant you the wisdom, words, and actions that would likely render your prayers and warfare acceptable to Him. Then bring yourself, your church, your city, and your assignment the fullest measure of victory and glory – giving the Kingdom of God the clear advantage over the enemy.

Second Duty

Your second duty is to recruit a sufficient number of wailing men, women, and children to keep a steady and strong firewall against the enemy. Intercession should be done in troops. You must try to keep a steady group of intercessors praying at all times for the success of God's overall campaign. Satan takes no breaks, and neither should you. You must always be recruiting and training others to pray so as to prevent any decrease in spiritual momentum. Unless additional recruits are enrolled into prayer groups, the number will constantly dwindle, for some are bound to retire through old age, battle fatigue, or disinterest.

Third Duty

While the troops of intercessors are praying and working together, you must see that the intercessors get enough nourishment by the Word of God in order endure the labor-intensive work of prayer.

Intercessors are tied to the altars of God's work. If an intercessor does not have a healthy diet of the Word and personal worship, they can neither overtake the enemy or escape an ambush.

The intercessor must remain humble and able to take even the harshest of commands. They must remain modest, submissive, and honorable because disobedient intercessors assist the enemy more than they realize. **Rebellion has no place in the heart of an intercessor.** The enemy will always look for treason and will exploit that open area. A rebellious intercessor can cause more damage than the enemy.

Intercessors must be able to pray through rough patches. They must be able to ascend in warfare through accusations and condemnation, physical and emotional attacks, and unusually heavy terrain. An intercessor who tries to ascend in pain without healing their soul wounds is useless. They will never be able to travel into the deeper realms of prayer. Therefore, deliverance and healing must be a part of the respite plan for intercessors. We all need a break. Intercessors must be ordered to take a break before a breakdown occurs.

Intercessors must be able to pray through rough patches.

Moses' inability to deal with the rigors of leading people out of Egypt caused him to disobey God and it cost him entrance into the Promised Land as their leader. A tired or frustrated intercessor can fall victim to despair and offense just like anyone else. When they do, it's like leaving the keys to your car in the door for anyone to enter and drive until they crash, dismantle the car and sell it for parts—or they are arrested.

WE MUST HAVE EMOTIONALLY HEALTHY TROOPS FOR WARFARE.

The Next Order of Business

Having made sure the troops of intercessors are in good condition, the next business is to train them how to ascend and descend in prayer. For many, their knowledge of prayer has been to just open your mouth and go. They must learn to cover themselves properly before they engage spiritual activity. Teach them that we owe our lives and the safety of our families to knowing how to properly apply the protection of God before any spiritual engagement. They must be taught to protect themselves from wounds and offenses.

They have the greatest chance of inflicting mortal wounds to the enemy when they themselves are healed and healthy. They must have regular target practice praying over all sorts of subjects, since any area may become the area of warfare. As soon as they have acquired a firm understanding of the ***A.R.M.E.D*** sequence, your next task is to make sure as many intercessors as possible are to be able to PRAY AND HIT THE TARGET when engaged. Make sure everyone becomes efficient in all the details of warfare.

For ensuring proficiency in spiritual matters, the cavalry commander, which is the senior leader, **is the principal authority**. This is the order of God. However, it is difficult for the senior leader to carry out all of these duties single-handedly. Therefore, we must select **lead** intercessors of the troops to assist him and charge them with the duty of taking a share in the management prayer teams. Those leaders should be as devoted to the mission as the senior leader and should have suitable spokesmen for the overall mission. They should be able to sound the alarm for prayer and have the troops respond swiftly and decisively when it comes to prayer assignments.

In Conclusion

Finally, intercession is often a nameless, faceless, and thankless cloak and dagger mission. Most people are unaware of the work intercessors do behind the scenes. We are secret assassins who often do the type of work that cannot be discussed often times.

There should be a public acknowledgement, sincere gratitude, and honor shown to these soldiers who keep the enemy at bay while many are asleep. Yes, we all should pray but sadly that is not yet the case. Until then, we must acknowledge the work of the intercessor as being vital to the success of The Kingdom of God.

Intercessors are history makers. They ensure that the plans and the purposes of God prevail. We **should all *deeply* appreciate their service.**

NOTES & REFERENCES

1. Billy Graham, *Angels: God's Secret Angels* (Published September 1975, Doubleday Books 0385113072, ISBN13: 9780385113076)

2. Dr. D.K. Olukoya, *Prayer Rain* (Published 1999, The Presshouse Publishing, Lagos, Nigeria, ISBN: 9789782947147)

3. https://www.cfaith.com/index.php/blog/23-articles/victory/19102-get-gods-perspective-on-the-unseen-realm

4. http://www.battlefocused.org/spiritualwarfare/matrix/

5. https://www.biblegateway.com/

6. https://mikebickle.org/articles/pdfs/Key_Apostolic_Prayers_and_Intercessory_Promises.pdf

7. https://biblehub.com/

8. https://sites.google.com/site/5rf6ghy3sw4d/download-in-pdf-the-unseen-realm-recovering-the-supernatural-worldview-of-the-bible-by---michael-s-heiser-full-books

9. https://www.blueletterbible.org/

10. https://www.beliefnet.com/inspiration/angels/what-are-the-9-orders-of-angels.aspx

11. https://www.defense.gov/Resources/Insignias/

ABOUT THE AUTHOR

Karen Bettis-Davis is an international, apostolic-prophetic general who ministers, equips, and teaches globally. As the product of a military family, she is no stranger to the art of strategic warfare, order, and protocol. She has decades of leadership experience in both the corporate and kingdom sectors.

Apostle Karen Bettis-Davis and her husband, Pastor DeWayne Davis, are founders of The Embassy Church located in Fredericksburg, VA. They, like Isaiah, have been concealed in His hands like "select arrows" that He is now releasing to His body for such a time as this. The message that she decrees is not only relevant but it is accompanied with an apostolic and prophetic edge that makes it both visible and attainable.

Ministry begins at home, as Apostle Karen is a wife, and mother to two treasured sons; Krystopher and Kealey. These two are a source of great joy. Apostle Karen and Pastor DeWayne are most proud of their son's tenderness towards the things of God. Apostle Karen holds seats on several boards that facilitate community healing. She has a governmental anointing that God has used to render justice at both the local and state levels. Apostle Karen is a Watchmen with The Family Research Council and has been honored to pray for and with Senators and Congressman laboring in Washington DC.

The Embassy encourages this generation to be the solution for their schools, community, and the world at large. Apostle Karen has served as a Director of Fredericksburg/Rappahannock Evangelical Alliance (FREA); an alliance of pastors who come together to see the Glory of God manifest in our region. She has founded a grassroots effort for women in ministry called **#Girlsmakegreatgeneralstoo.**

For more information, booking, and training sessions:
www.kbdavisworldwide.com